Shhhh! it's a Secret. How to Compete Against Walmart and the Internet.

Fran Tabor

Published by Elaine's Dreams, 2022.

SHHHH! IT'S A SECRET. HOW TO COMPETE AGAINST WALMART AND THE INTERNET.

First edition. July 26, 2022.

ISBN: 979-8201039271

Written by Fran Tabor.

Table of Contents

Life is a great teacher. I am thankful for every experience I've had...
especially those lessons that were most painful.

What this book isn't:
Basic money management; go to your accountant.
Get rich quick; don't believe in it.
Complete; learning never ends.
What this book is:
Fourteen Articles full of Attitude
Plus a few common sense ideas to help us all stay in the profit groove—no matter how much the nightly news tries to turn us survivors into quitters!

•

SHHHH! IT'S A SECRET
HOW TO COMPETE AGAINST WALMART AND THE INTERNET
Business Survival Tips for the 21st Century
Fran Tabor

This is dedicated to my parents, who taught me that what others call failure is really an educational experience.

The greater the education, the more expensive it usually is—and it is entirely up to me to get my money's worth out of all life's lessons.

Fletchers and Dodo Birds

SHOULD ANYONE NEED to get out of a comfortable chair, drive through obnoxious traffic, find a parking place just to buy stuff?

Some insist, "No. Brick & mortar retailers are the Dodo birds of business, as extinct as the town fletcher, the arrow maker."

Most Americans' knowledge of bows & arrows is limited to box store toys. Few know the arrow is still being invented, that archery enthusiasts live everywhere. Most big cities have archery specialty stores.

Fifty years ago, a modern fletcher had two choices. He could cater only to local cliental or risk investing in expensive catalogues. Today, the net lets any fletcher create an on-line catalogue to sell his wares around the world. Growth is limited by talent, not a fat bankroll.

Some archery dealers have abandoned their stores to the net. Others use the Internet to explain why archery equipment should be personalized and draw people into their stores to a level never before possible.

What does this have to do with your specialty shop?

Everything.

Too often our potential customers aren't even aware of anything beyond box store choices. In the past, it took big money to let people know we independent specialty shops exist, and what we offer that box stores can't.

Just when the Internet made it easier to go against the retail giants, it also made it more dangerous.

You take your time to educate your customer about what choices best fit her exact needs—and believe you will make a big sale, the kind that pays the rent. Your customer is thrilled to finally have his needs met. The anticipated profit is your payment for educating your customer.

Then the customer researches the net, buys the item at cost and an undeserving stranger gets paid for YOUR work!

Should we whine "There's no way to compete with the net!" and just quit?

If we sell _only_ product that people already know about, perhaps we should.

If we sell _only_ product readily available elsewhere, perhaps we should.

If, when teaching about new products, we do nothing to make our store's product different from our competitor's, again, perhaps we should just wave "Good by!" to our customer, abandon him to the net.

What can ANY brick and mortar business offer that the Internet can't?

First, we are time savers.

In many of our ads, I mention, "We research so YOU don't have too." Do you think most people LIKE researching? Or would they rather be emailing friends? Playing games? Watching movies?

Secondly, **we are safer**.

Mention the _safety_ of "try before you buy." Share horror stories about customers who phoned for help from uncaring, out-of-state, internet dealers who really don't care.

We, on the other hand, often see our customers at the local grocery store. We MUST care.

Worse, to discourage returns, most Internet dealers make the customer pay for return shipping. What value is a guarantee if the seller knows he will seldom—if ever—have to honor it?

Thirdly, we can customize.

Plus we have another Big Advantage over Internet shops.

Remember the archery stores? Once their customers learn the advantage of trial shooting, they want to touch, feel, smell and—most importantly—shoot a prospective new piece.

Any demonstration on the net or TV will never be as trusted as a person's own touchy-feely experience. We show, not tell, what makes our merchandise special.

The final emphasis should always be on feelings, something the net can't match.

It is an honest final emphasis because people will like and recommend products only if they feel good using them.

Are our brick and mortar stores the Dodo birds of the business world?

Dodo birds never learned to change their life style when hungry sailors changed their world.

Modern fletchers, unlike Dodo birds, learned and are wealthier than their medieval predecessors.

The choice is up to each of us—to learn or to become a dodo bird.

Life with Blinders Off

A FRIEND ASKED ME, "With all that is going wrong with the economy, with all the bad stuff that's happened to you, why don't you quit? There's still a shortage of math teachers."

Have any of your friends asked:

"Isn't it dangerous to own a small business?"

"How can you live, not knowing from one week to the next how much money you'll make?'

"Why don't you get a real job?"

Or have bankers ever told you:

"We don't like to loan to business owners. Their income is too uncertain."

When we first started our small business, we often heard that one, as our "secure" employees more easily obtained loans. Their income was no more "secure" than our business.

Have you heard politicians expound on how:

"People can't function unless they know they will always have a home and a 'reasonable' standard of living."

News commentators talk about, "these times of economic uncertainty" as though economic uncertainty were something new.

To small business owners across America, what their neighbors see as new, for us has been daily life from the first day we decided to be self-employed.

Our employed neighbors wonder how we can handle the risks. When a recession hits, our "safely employed" neighbors discover, often too late, that their paychecks are only as good as the profitability of their employer.

We small business owners and self-employed people have no more risk than they. It is just that we have always known we were at risk.

Back in the horse and buggy days, one of the greatest dangers came from unexpected side motions. A gust of wind sending leaves swirling could make a horse bolt fearfully, putting horse, cart and humans at risk. To prevent panic, buggy drivers put blinders on the horse so he couldn't see anything but a safe road straight ahead.

This prevented unwarranted panic, but it also blinded the horse from real danger.

In the same way, the average employed person has been conned into thinking that he is "safe", an attitude shared by many financial institutions.

The average person is told daily that life should have safety nets for every possible calamity, as though real life can be devoid of danger.

We small business owners are eyes-wide-open buggy drivers; not draft horses wearing blinders.

As Jim Collins said in his April 2009 <u>Inc</u> article "...My students use to come to me at Stanford and say, 'I'd really like to do something on my own, but I'm just not ready to take that much risk. So I took the job with IBM.' And I would say, 'You're not ready for risk? What's the first thing you learn about investing? Never put all your eggs in one basket. You've just put all your eggs in one basket **that is held by somebody else.**'

As an entrepreneur, you know what the risks are. You see them. You understand them. You manage them. If you join someone else's company, you may not know those risks, and not because they don't exist...that's a much more exposed position*...."

People confuse predictability with safety and uncertainty with risks.

What we business owners have is the ability to face uncertainty, to have faith life will average out. Because we are not relying on one person to provide our livelihood, we are at less risk than any employee who relies on his boss.

Because we can see the big picture, we are not as shocked when disaster strikes.

It important for us to remember that our employed neighbors feel more secure only because they are living life with their economic blinders on.

The employee thinks he can see a safe road ahead.

We are the drivers who see the entire road, with all its dangers.

We live with our economic blinders off.

I am self-employed because anything else is too risky.

*emphasis mine

The Tortoise, the Hare

&

Those Expensive, Time-Consuming Trade Conventions

WE'VE ALL HEARD THE tale of the tortoise and the hare.

The lowly tortoise challenged the Hare to a marathon. The hare agreed and they took off.

After a long run in the hot sun, the hare decided he needed a little siesta under a shady tree.

Dare he risk the break? The tortoise was a distant speck; the finish line, only a sprint away. Of course he could!

Cool shade, a soft warm breeze, gentle bird song...the hare slept deeply. An hour later, the tortoise plodded past the still sleeping hare. After another hour the excited cheers from the watching crowd awoke the hare—the tortoise was just feet from the finish line.

The hare charged forward, faster than he'd ever run before, only to arrive seconds too late.

The moral Aesop gave was "slow and steady wins the race."

But there is another, more important moral:

The wise race against someone better themselves.

If the hare had raced against another hare, or a road runner, or a cheetah (Now there's motivation!), win or loose he would have run a good race.

Everything we do is a race.

We "race" to gather money faster than our creditors want it.

We race to accumulate savings "faster" than we will live.

We race with our competitors, including COSTCO and Wal-Mart, to earn the right to serve our customers.

And we "race" to become a better person.

How good a race we run is as influenced by the quality of our follow racers as it is by our ability.

Low ability that continuously pits itself against high ability will astound their detractors by eventually doing well.

High ability that decides that hard work is not necessary, risks waking up and discovering the race is lost.

In every field, those at the top agree on one bit of advice: If you want to get better, hang around already successful people.

And every truly successful professional I've met has also shared another life lesson: Until you've helped others learn to succeed, you haven't done anything worthwhile.

What does that have to do with those inconvenient, often expensive, conventions?

Those who take time out from operating their business to learn more, tend to be the best in the field. It is a true opportunity to associate with those top performers—to race with hares not tortoises.

When we encounter others on the convention floor, it is also our opportunity to share what we've learned.

No matter what you business specialty, there is bound to be an organization for it.

Don't know of one? Look up your business on the Internet and add 'organizations' to your search.

Can't find one? Check out related blog sites and ask.

Still can't find one?

All organizations started with one person. Perhaps, for your specialty, that person will be you.

How strongly do I believe professional trade shows are worth the time and money? Consider an article I wrote for *The Floor Care Professional* following a trade convention in Los Vegas...

What Happens in Vegas...

"IF YOU DON'T READ NEWSPAPERS, you are uninformed. If you do read them, you are misinformed" Mark Twain.

In the spirit of Mark Twain:

"If you don't follow the news, you won't know which business plans to make.

If you are informed, you'll be too scared to stay in business." (me)

Pontificating experts saturate our news with stories that compare American small business to a boxer sinking to the floor from a knock-out punch.

How do those experts think struggling businesses should respond? By waiting for someone else to rescue them!

As the keynote speaker said, none of us are getting a government bail out.

At the convention we got something better: ways to fight back by working *smarter*!

Dealers came from every part of the country.

Both jokes and business plans were shared.

One lady described buying out a competitor's old-time, grime-filled vac shop. She cleaned, updated and painted it; transforming the old vac shop into a popular and profitable Vacuum Store.

During the Friday appreciation time, I talked with several men who successfully used the Internet to drive business into their stores.

Another man told me how (inspired by yours truly) he is now known as a cleaning expert. Women now come to his store to ask advice; and buy recommended problem solvers.

Booths were crammed with a plethora of merchandise.

Vacuum attachments that had looked over-rated in the catalogs were experienced first hand—and ordered.

From the opening awards presentation, to the final minutes Saturday noon, the VDTA show was a celebration of success.

What happened in VDTA/SDTA Vegas—the new demo ideas, the new products, the mutual encouragement—did not stay in Vegas.

We took it home.

Communities Need Repair Shops...

If they want a stronger economy

WHEN PROFESSIONAL CITY planners try to think of everything a community needs, they seldom consider humble repair shops. Some cities even zone them out of "nice" areas. Yet repair shops create dollars-in-circulation, our economic life-blood.

Consider what happens to two vacuum owners, each with a $100 in his pocket, both mechanically challenged, when their vacuums choke on one mystery chunk too many.

The man who lives in a town without a repair shop most likely tosses his old vacuum and buys a new one from a local box store. When he spends his $100, about $90 leaves his community. Whoosh! Gone!

His wallet is left empty.

Life is a challenge.

Now consider a lucky man who took his choked up vacuum to a repair shop, and spent $50 getting it running as good as new.

All of that $50 stayed in the community.

On his way home, he stops at a local coffee shop, spends $10.00. About $8.00 will stay in the community.

When he gets home, his wife says, "Let's go to the farmer's market. I've heard there're some great plants!" They go buy plants. All that money stays in the community.

On their way home, they pick up milk. That evening, he still has enough change in his pocket to be lunch money for his son.

Because he had a repair shop to go to, over $90 stayed in his community, his kid had milk for his morning cereal and money for lunch. His wife is happy. Life is good.

Few enter the repair business because of the glamour of working with broken appliances. Or go into alternations & mending because we like sewing on old clothes. Or any of the other you-messed it-up so I'll-fix-it-up businesses.

We simply wanted to provide an honest living for our families.

Our unglamorous businesses help our neighbors prosper. Because of us, everyone is able to afford a little more luxury.

But can anyone make a good living in such humble professions? Consider the following excerpt from <u>Live Abundantly! Business Lessons from the Bible</u>, lesson twenty-six.

Background:

Joseph, a foreign slave in Egypt, became Pharaoh's right hand man by predicting seven years of plentiful harvest to be followed by seven years of severe drought and famine.

Being forewarned, Pharaoh stored more than enough grain to last during the lean years. When the famine hit, he sold the stored grain to both his subjects and starving neighboring peoples. Every year of the famine, the price went up, making Pharaoh much wealthier than before.

The drought drove Joseph's family to seek grain in Egypt. When Joseph recognized his brothers among the hundreds who came pleading for grain, he told them if they left the deserts and return with his father and their families, he would give them all they needed.

Humble all the way to the bank

WHEN JOSEPH'S FAMILY came to Egypt, it wasn't just his twelve brothers and father; it was the whole tribe; their wives, many children, servants, huge flocks and herds. It would have seemed like a small invasion.

When the citizens of Egypt were starving, to see that many strangers and animals given the best, could have bred resentment. Even "divine" pharaohs were known to meet untimely deaths when they became too unpopular.

Joseph wisely forestalled such resentment before it started.

*...When Pharaoh shall say...What is your occupation? That ye shall say ...cattle...for every shepherd is an abomination unto the Egyptians.**

How could lowly shepherds be worth an Egyptian's notice? How fortunate Joseph's family could take over a necessary but disdainful occupation, freeing the Egyptians from dirtying their hands.

His family's herds and wealth grew.

There can be great profit in activities others consider beneath them.

**Genesis 46:33-34*

Teaching Employees to Sell

Showing Love

"LOVE YOUR CUSTOMERS and the money will follow." Bob Negen

"No one will care how much you know, until they know how much you care." Zig Zigler

Customers are going to decide if they <u>want</u> to buy from you in the first minute. How, in less than sixty seconds, can we show a customer we love and care about them?

More accurately, how can we get our customers to become instantly infatuated with us?

Let's go to the "Instant love" experts: Hollywood.

Instant-infatuation is love Hollywood style. Remember all those "first attraction" scenes? Most are pretty much the same.

The hero looks at the beautiful lady; the lady returns his look. They stare intently at each other...the longer their eyes lock, the more we know they are "interested."

Movie makers know that real caring is expressed with direct eye contact, followed by silent reaction BEFORE anything is said...unless the hero is a Jerry Lewis style love-klutz. The Klutzes start talking (or stammering) *immediately.*

Selling Klutzes also yammer immediately. That split-second of silence makes them nervous. They "know" they can't accomplish anything while standing silent.

How wrong!

Much happens when people are silent, all of it important.

Great actors know that their reaction to others is as important—often MORE important—than their own lines. Doubt that? Rent some of the early Schwarzenegger films. He could barely speak English, but could he stare and react!

Lots of forgotten actors had bodies and ambition as great as his, but few mastered his silent stares.

As sales people, we get to practice silent looks, only with a smile!

First, notice your customer's body language.

Match it!

People feel most at ease with someone like themselves, and matching body language will say "We are soul mates."—even if you are different genders, cultures or racial groups. (Clinical research psychology should be part of every salesman's reading.)

When your customer describes his situation, don't rush to say, "I know just what you need!" especially if you believe you do.

Instead, pause. (Think early Schwarzenegger, he ALWAYS paused before saying anything important.) Look directly into your customer's eyes; give a slight "yes" nod.

How long a pause? In proportion to the importance of the request.

Low ticket item, <u>very</u> briefly, then solve the immediate problem.

After that if you wish to introduce a higher ticket item, again look her in the eye, longer pause because you are thinking of something important JUST For HER.

At this point, clerks will TELL the customer about something else to buy.

Just telling someone "You also need this cool thing I am selling." is giving unsolicited advice.

We have all received unasked for advice from our parents, teachers and significant others.

Do you like being told what to do?

Are our customers any different?

Isn't unasked for advice sometimes called nagging?

Crash and burn infomercials may get away with it, but when dealing with someone one to one, "buy this now" is harsh.

We must show our customers that we love them, not that we can bludgeon them into buying more.

If we shouldn't force-tell the customers about another item, what can we do?

For the last few thousand years, mothers have been telling their daughters "If you want a man to 'discover' he is interested in you, ask him about himself."

Ask a question related to something the customer just purchased.

Example: She just bought thread or fabric.

You: "How long have you had your sewing machine?"... "The last time you had it serviced?"

If it's over two years, a worried pause, "Oh", said slowly. Maintain eye contact, stay quiet.

If she just bought filters, substitute vacuum for sewing machine.

If your customer just bought printing supplies or a computer component, same questions.

Give her a chance to ask why you are worried.

Only if you are silent long enough can the customer realize you are concerned and then **ask you** why you are worried.

Your direct eye contact told her your care.

Your silence gives her a chance to respond, to feel in control.

Most important, your silence keeps you from being a pushy, nagging salesperson.

An open-ended silence also lets you easily segue into either selling a maintenance service or a new item.

The more expensive the item or service the customer asks about, the longer the pause should be. She is pondering spending a considerable amount of money.

She deserves consideration from you.

Nothing says consideration like being polite.

It is polite to let the other person talk first.

It is respectful to be attentive when spoken to. If you repeat back to her what she said, she knows you were attentive.

Example:

In response to your questions, your customer has just told you his never-been-serviced computer is five years old. Instead of declaring, "You are overdue for a professional cleaning!" as though the customer were a wayward child and you the demanding parent, try, in concerned, not shocked, tones:

"Your computer's over 5 years old and never been professional cleaned?"

Then silently wait for a response.

You now have the beginning of a beautiful friendship. But what about letting her know you are an expert?

Proverbs 18:28 *Even a fool, when he holdeth his peace, is counted wise: And he that shutteth his lips is esteemed a man of understanding.*

The same thoughtful silence that lets your customer feel in control also makes you look like an expert.

Now it is up to you to be the expert she expects.

Teaching Employees Selling

Sharing Love

LIFE WAS ONCE SIMPLE. You were self-employed.

If a customer came in, and he bought something, you ate.

If he didn't, you didn't eat.

As you learned to sell, your customers spent more money. Your business grew. Now it is no longer possible for you to do everything.

A lone self-employed person is a job-owner, not a business owner. The moment you become an employer, you join the ranks of business owners. Most new business owners hire someone else to do the "safe jobs," that don't directly affect your income, such as bookkeeping.

Your most important, greatest income producing job is selling the services and/or products you offer.

You don't dare entrust that to anyone...or do you?

Wouldn't it be nice to be on vacation, and know you are not missing income opportunities?

It's easy to teach someone to work a till, stock shelves and keep your retail space dusted. (Side note: Any front person who won't help with the cleaning should be fired. Immediately.)

It is not easy to teach a neophyte to take someone from wanting *cheap* and leading him to a high end purchase.

Can we shorten the training process?

You and I know that each customer who comes through your door is precious.

People who have always worked for others are often deluded into thinking it doesn't matter how much the customer spends. Good day, slow day, they eat the same.

Ask you employees, "Who is the most valuable person in the store? Who gives you your paycheck?"

The only correct answer: "The customer!"

The first, and most important, lesson to teach?

Each customer is a precious diamond in the rough.

When diamonds first come out of the ground, they don't look or feel like diamonds. They need to be cleaned and cut to become the sparkling gems on display within the lighted jeweler's case. Any misstep from the stone's first discovery to the finished mounting can result in a valuable gem becoming worthless.

Customers are the same.

The customer always deserves our best—our best appearance, speech, manners and knowledge.

Even Wal-Mart trains people to be clerks.

Selling is much more than clerking; it takes an apprenticeship period to learn it.

To the customer, your selling apprentice will look like a clerk. The clerk/apprentice must be trained on the physical basics of what you sell before he starts clerking. If absolutely no one else is available, he can do an educational presentation to the customer. At all other times the apprentice <u>must</u> request help.

Getting help is not shouting "Hey, Bob, a guy's here to buy a vacuum!"

That kind of request can cost you a sale.

Instead, teach your apprentice to confide to the customer, "I'm just learning about this too. Let me get an expert to help<u> us</u>." Then quickly get the best salesperson available.

When the apprentice returns with your expert, he/she should have a well-rehearsed ten second introduction sharing how wonderful your expert is. "This is—, he has thirty years of experience." Or whatever his best-sounding attribute is.

At this point, your beginner can give a brief summation of all he has learned about the customer's needs/wants. Then pauses, lets your expert salesperson greet the customer.

The only reason your sales-trainee should leave the presentation is to answer a phone or help another customer; if called away, the apprentice should return as soon as practical.

Learning to be a great salesperson is more important than stocking shelves, cleaning or doing paperwork.

Where and how the apprentice stands is of vital importance.

If he stands next to your expert salesperson, they will be identified together. Your customer will perceive it as two salespeople against him. If your customer is a woman, and they are both men, it can trigger instinctive wariness.

As soon as your apprentice has finished giving <u>The Very Positive Introduction</u>, he should step away from your master salesperson, and next to the customer. Physically and emotionally your customer and your apprentice are now on the same side. Your customer will feel safer.

If your apprentice assumes the same posture (Are hands in front, back, or in pockets? Feet positioned similarly?) as the customer, it will reinforce your customer's identification with him.

Your apprentice is now a selling aid.

First, he is a **mood setter**.

Have you ever watched a comedy in a crowed theater? Notice how if one person smiles at a mildly humorous scene, than another will chuckle; soon the whole crowd is laughing? We humans pick up on the mood of the people around us.

It is now your apprentice's job to listen, to believe every word you speak is *fascinating*. His conversation with the customer should be minimal, ideally no more than a thoughtful nod, or a brief answer to a direct question, then again giving rapt attention to your master salesperson.

If your store gives any commission credit, it can be a good idea to pay a commission to a cooperative apprentice. That can help prevent people trying to swim when they should still be wearing water wings—in other words, a few extra learning dollars can prevent loosing big ticket sales.

After the customer has left, it is tempting to immediately discuss the educational presentation—the sale.

Don't.

Your first question after the customer leaves should be "What did you like best about her?"

Why?

The first lesson, the customer is precious, must be continuously reinforced.

Too often our society teaches us to look for the negative. If we focus on the negative in anyone and anything, we see it as less valuable and less likeable. The more your employee likes and values his customers, the better he will be able to relate to them.

<u>What we are asked about, we will look for.</u>

This will teach your employee to look for the nicest, most likeable characteristics in each customer.

He will learn to see each one as a valuable, precious human being; and the rare you-know-what as the aberrations they are.

Looking for the customer's most likeable qualities will help him to see the customer as precious more than customer-as-income lectures ever will.

We all want our friends to have good things

If what you are selling is a benefit to your customers, and your employees learn to value and like your customers, they will want each customer to have the benefits your business can offer them. It's the loving thing to do.

This team-selling apprenticeship period is more than teaching product knowledge—that can be learned reading or watching a video—it's to teach attitude and physical nuance.

The second benefit to having the apprentice stand next to the customer? So he can watch and learn from the customer's vantage point.

Short-Changed Customer

Short Changes the Till

"HI, I'D LIKE TO BUY a (Brand X vacuum)."

A sparkling new (Brand X) set on my floor. "Here's one. Is this the model you were thinking of?"

"Yes. I've got lots of thick carpet, allergies and pets. My neighbor said this is the best."

From experience, I knew the model she was looking at was a terrible choice for anyone with thick carpet and pets. I described its negative features.

She crinkled her nose in disgust. "Yuck. What would you recommend?"

Confident that she recognized my expertise, I went straight to the demo floor, showed her a model I liked and told her how it better fit her needs. She pushed it across the floor. She liked it how gobbled up the fake fur (kapok).

"This seems perfect. How much did you say it was?"

I repeated the price.

"That's a hundred less than I planned to spend! I'll take it."

Minutes later I was carrying her new vacuum out to her car, wishing all sales could be that fast.

The next day, she was back with another lady. Both women glowered at me as though I were on America's most wanted. "You sold me a no good vacuum. I want my money back."

"What's the problem?"

"After vacuuming, my neighbor," She nodded at the woman with her. "Brought over her (Brand X vacuum), and picked up more dirt. You said any problems, I could bring it back. I have a problem with <u>you</u>. You lied. Here's your machine, I want my money."

I was hurt...The cash register quivered in anticipated pain.

"Uh, what happened when you then vacuumed again with your new vacuum?"

The buyer looked confused, then thoughtful.

Her neighbor glared. "We didn't bother!"

The buyer regained her tough stance. "Right!"

Another salesperson watched me flounder under their double-header attack. He approached slowly.

"Hi, I see this didn't do an adequate job for you." as though in total agreement.

The friend interrupted. "She doesn't need another sales pitch; just give her money back!"

My fellow salesman looked first at her, then the buyer as he replied, "We just want you to get the vacuum that best suits both your cleaning needs _and_ your budget. Can you tell me a little about the carpet it was used on?"

He gets a detailed description. He looks thoughtful. Silence, then, "Many people with your carpet type are satisfied with one of these." He walks over to the same vacuum she had first wanted and picks it up.

He paused. "Do you also have pet hair or does any one in your family have long hair?"

"Yes! My daughters, cats and dogs all shed."

"Oh." He looked worried, said nothing.

She breaks the silence. "Is that a problem?"

"For this machine, yes. Would you like to see why? It will only take a minute."

Carrying the brand X vacuum, he walks over to the demo floor. The ladies follow.

He shows them the brush roll, explains how it is made. He picks up a similar, worn-out brush roll, shows what dirt and hair did to it. He has them feel the brushes on both the new and worn out Brand X brush roll.

He then hands them a metal brush roll, explains the construction, discusses the advantages to replaceable strips.

Salt is poured onto the floor. Using a manual carpet sweeper, he shows how brush action without suction can clean.

Then he pulls out our favorite brand. Another salt line is poured onto the floor; a quarter is placed beyond the salt.

"You saw how cleaning can be done with no suction. This vacuum" He picks up a step-down from the model my customer bought. "Has a smaller motor than yours. It has less hose suction than a new (Brand X) vacuum. Let's compare <u>carpet</u> cleaning."

He vacuums a third of the salt line with the Brand X, admires the 'excellent' performance. He vacuums up to the quarter, and back. The quarter sits there.

He vacuums a third of the salt line with the step-down vacuum. It vibrates towards the vacuum. He goes up to the quarter. It jiggles into the vacuum.

He SHOWED what I only told.

Her friend is gradually persuaded that maybe our vacuum is *almost* as good as her Brand X vacuum—but only almost.

My customer says thank you for the information, but she wants to look around more, give it some thought.

I knew she wouldn't be buying the Brand X, but she will be checking other vacuums for the features she now knows she needs.

I "cheerfully" refunded her money. I could hear the cash register sob.

If instead of a rushed, mostly-talking demonstration, I had let her hold both brush rolls; encouraged her to vacuum with both the Brand X and my recommendation; had her examine the agitator; **if I had not short-changed her**; she would have understood which vacuum best fit her needs.

The decision to buy would have been hers; not the result of some salesperson yammering on.

My customer would have had the ability to show her neighbor the obvious advantages of her new vacuum over the Brand X vacuum. And she would still own it.

Even better, her neighbor may have come in, pre-primed to like us, asking about the cool vacuum.

My short-cut "selling" had cost not just the one sale, but referral sales as well.

Three l-o-n-g weeks later.

My customer came in alone. She asked if she could give our favorite brand a second test drive.

This time she kept it.

No matter what we are selling, if our customers are to stay sold, it is important to show more than tell what sets our products apart.

Our words are forgotten, and too often misunderstood.

What is experienced is both better remembered and better understood.

What Couldn't be Given Away at $200,

Sells like Hotcakes at $2,500!

ABRIDGED FROM INC. January 2009 Legacy article, p.120:

Mr. James Benson, solar power pioneer, SpaceDev, Inc. founder, and hybrid motor supplier for the first privately funded manned space flight; died October 2008 at the young age of 63.

Mr. Bensen was a man who dreamed of commercial space travel. His financial success developing Compusearch software helped him to indulge that dream.

Compusearch, an excellent product, almost failed.

Why?

Because of the most common error of all beginning salespeople: selling too low.

"...In 1983, he co-founded Compusearch, which produced software...Benson had no luck {selling his program} until a prospect explained that the $200 software seemed too inexpensive to do what it claimed. 'He raised the price to $2,500, and it started to sell like hotcakes,'..."

(emphasis mine)

Before the customer enlightened him, did Mr. Benson believe he wasn't a salesman?

Or that others "out there" with bigger development budgets had better software?

Perhaps Benson believed no one bought because he didn't know enough of the "right" people?

Since he couldn't sell his software at $200, did he ever offer it at $190?

James Benson knew Compusearch was good. He knew it was needed. He knew he could explain it. He just could not sell it.

Mr. Benson made the classic error of underestimating his own value.

Just like thousands of small business owners do every day.

When we sell a repair to our customer what we are selling is our expertise.

Our customers do not know how to judge an unknown repairman...just like Mr. Benson's first customers did not know how to evaluate his unknown software. They instead **trust us to tell them what our value is.**

If one shop advertises "Full Service, Only $19.95" and another just as boldly advertises "Full service, $49.95", most of us will believe the half-priced service is a half-quality service. The lower priced shop will have less credibility.

The same is even more true when it comes to complex skills—such as computer programming.

In both the VacDealers Forum and VacHeads Forum, dealers have discussed how raising repair rates increased both customer confidence and the owner's income.

"Drop the price, loose the sale" is equally true on the sales floor.

Imagine you are a customer, listening to a salesman selling you an appliance that is normally $1400, but is on sale today for "Only $1200." You are thinking *"It looks awesome. Thanks to his great demonstration, I've learned it has the features I want. But how to afford it? I came in planning to spend $300, now I'm considering spending four times that much...Dare I write a check? Use a credit card? What will my family say?"*

As you attempt to sort your thoughts, the salesman keeps yakity-yakking. Finally, he's quiet.

You can think.

The salesman interrupts again. "If you buy today, you can have it for another $200 off, only $999."

You think *"Whoa, I almost paid $1200! It's a good thing I kept my mouth shut, or this fast talker might have over-charged me. My family will ridicule me if I pay too much...I better stick to the three hundred dollar model...perhaps one of theirs, but I'm no longer sure they can be trusted."*

"That's a lot of money. I'll have to think about it."

To tell the person you no longer highly value his product would be insulting. You are too nice.

Just like Mr. Benson's first few dozen prospects didn't wish to offend him by saying his software couldn't be any good because it was too cheap.

Knowing human nature, I can guarantee at least a few who didn't buy the "too cheap" software, said, "James, I would love to give Compusearch a try, but we just don't have an extra $200 in our budget this year. Maybe next time."

Mr. Benson would have left the office, thinking, "My price was too high."

If you believe what you are offering is more valuable than the competition's, then back your beliefs with action.

Charge more.

When the customer pauses, don't assume he thinking "That's way too much money." Don't crash into his thoughtful silence with a "Today only!" offer.

A better way to handle the customer who needs to think?

First, never delude yourself into believing you are a mind reader. Mr. Benson's customers were thinking, "No way a program that cheap can be worth buying." while he assumed they were thinking, "Way too much money!"

Second, give your customer opportunities to think.

Every time you present new information, be silent, let him digest it.

If he still looks puzzled after a second of silence, he is either thinking of applications or still trying to decipher what your words. An open-ended but positive leaning question will help reveal which it is. "Wouldn't that make life easier for you?" often works.

Third, give him something physical to do, and keep quiet while he is doing it.

For instance, when showing a high end vacuum, say, "The physical fit to you is important. Just like two different people will disagree about which car drives better, people will disagree about which vacuum is the most pleasurable to use. Here, just vacuum awhile, go under furniture, use the tools. Any new questions, just ask."

Then take several steps away.

If you're a jeweler, you might hand your client two stones, saying, "Hold them up to the light. See which color you like best," then silently lean away.

This gives your customer a chance to collect his thoughts. If he is trying it, he wants it. When he is through handling your products, you can discuss what he likes and dislikes about each one.

Since nothing man-made is 100% perfect, allow him to decide which compromises he is willing to make. Too often, we salespeople—made nervous by the silence—suggest the compromises we think are the most logical.

If instead we respond to the customer's comments with defining questions or information, then HE owns the compromise, not us.

A common compromise at our store is new versus new warranty but almost new merchandise.

We ask if he would rather have a brand new vacuum, assembled just for him, or save twenty five dollars on the floor model. Most floor models have been used only in our store for vacuum demonstrations, with less than 5 hours total run time. They've never been sold and have a 100% manufacture's warranty.

It always shocks new employees how many people who could "barely afford to eat," suddenly turn their noses up at the discounted floor model, and instead choose to pay the full asking price for their new vacuum.

The higher-priced vacuum has more value to them—just like the higher priced program had more value to Mr. James Benson's customers.

Should additional discounts prove necessary, find a way that does not devalue your new merchandise. Trade-ins are a common venue. Another is to offer a fully serviced and warranted rental unit at a discount. Another is to say, "I know you will benefit from all the features you've seen, but if you had to, which one can you do without? Perhaps, by eliminating what you don't need as much, we can lower the price." In other words, the discussion is back to compromises, not to-buy or not-to-buy.

What you do not, ever, compromise is your value.

Each person who chooses to pay your full price, is someone a too-quickly lowered price could have chased away.

Why chance it?

My $100,000 Customers

MOST PURCHASES IN MY small retail store are less than $50.00. We have a few high end vacuums, and a couple of very expensive sewing machines, but few of my customers collect expensive merchandise.

Yet I have several $100,000 customers.

The ladies who tie for this position have been customers of mine for over twenty years.

A La Betty Crocker (who was based on a composite of the Betty Crocker Company founders), this will be a composite history of:

My $100,000 customer

Let's call her Alice, because when her friends have any kind of cleaning question, they Go Ask Alice.

I first met Alice years ago when she was a newlywed. She & her husband had $50 in wedding gift money to buy a vacuum & had heard my radio ad "S-t-r-e-tch your vacuum dollar with Clean, Like New Vacuums!" They seemed like any other cash-strapped young couple. We stressed that the used vacuum would have a future higher trade-in value since they bought it from us, than if it had been purchased elsewhere.

Profit that day: Less that $5.00.

It turned out that Alice's parents needed a new vacuum. At her recommendation, they came in & bought a new, top of the line, Panasonic.

Her mother's church needed an extra vacuum. They bought one of our used ones, and then noticed we sold cleaning supplies.

The church started using our good smelling bathroom cleaner. The ladies at the church came in to buy the bathroom cleaner for their homes.

One of those ladies mentioned troubles with her new puppy...we sold her an effective live bacterial product. She sang its praises to everyone. All her friends with puddle-prone pets came to our store.

The next few years we sold Alice a better vacuum, at least ten vacuums to church members and a new commercial unit for the sanctuary, plus more cleaning supplies.

Seven years after their first visit, Alice & her husband still struggled to make ends meet. She decided to clean houses while her two children were in school. She came to us for help because we "taught her how to clean toilets" and she has loved her vacuum.

I advised her how to be more professional by such little things as write out in detail what she would do when housecleaning. If a customer wanted to pay her less, to say "OK, but which one of these items do you want me to leave out?" This hint alone became worth gold to her. It allowed her to honorably spend less time at homes that paid less, and more time in those willing to pay more.

Since she was now a professional, I allowed her to receive case lot rates for items purchased in smaller quantities. (She simply had no place to store larger quantities.)

Whenever I learned about a new technique or more about the chemistry of cleaning, I shared the knowledge.

In short, I helped her to make the transition from struggling amateur to profitable cleaning professional.

Only four years later she asked me to stop recommending her to new clients. She had more business than she could handle and was going to have to raise her rates—again—to cut down on the number of homes she and her employee (That's right, employee. She was now a successful business woman!) cleaned each week.

All of her clients are very successful people. They have to be to be able to afford her. At her recommendation, most of them have bought vacuums and cleaning supplies from me.

Thank you, Alice!

Now that I'm thinking about it, $100,000 is a conservative estimate for how much that first $50 sale was really worth.

I also made a life-long friend.

If you are thinking, 'That works for the cleaning supply business, but not mine.' you might be wrong.

What made Alice special wasn't just typical word-of-mouth. When she became a professional user of my products, people valued her words more than others. Likewise, those customers whose friends know them to be cleaning fanatics have more valuable word-of mouth than their "more casual living" acquaintances.

When I first met Alice, there was not a clue how important she would become to my business.

Everyone who comes into my shop is seen as a future Alice.

Specialty businesses have certain customers who use their services on a more extreme level than most. Whether it's the dedicated hobbyist or a professional end-user, it behooves us to offer special attention to our extreme customers.

We can tell them first about new products, offer special rates, find ways for them to succeed.

We need to become their treasure trove of information.

If in 1990 someone bought a stock for $50 a share, and in 2010 it was worth $100,000, would you think he was lucky? Or smart? Or both?

We have the opportunity to turn $50 customers into $100,000 customers every day—only luck has nothing to do with it.

The following article shares more information about this.

Your Store: As contagious as a pet rock?

ALL OF US STRIVE TO get good word-of-mouth advertising.

But the ugly truth is that if you have ninety-nine customers who are enthusiastic about how wonderful you are, and one person who thinks you are the scum of the earth, we all know who is going to do the most talking.

And which one will remember us the longest.

Most people have little reason to talk about vacuums, our main product. Social small talk is about movies, weather, politics, sports...vacuums come up as often —and for the same reason as—dentists. People talk about them only when they have a painful problem.

Our goal: Have happy customers who will talk about us with enthusiasm to lots of different people.

In Malcolm Gladwell's book <u>The Tipping Point</u>, he discusses how retail success and epidemics are similar. A product, like a contagious disease, can exist in small, unnoticed quantities until suddenly a small change occurs that has a BIG effect. It can happen to anything.

When I was a teenager, it happened to pet rocks. (For you youngsters out there: I am not making this up. Ask your elders about pet rocks.)

It can happen to your store.

Think of your store's popularity as an epidemic you want to get started. According to Gladwell's Law of the Few, there are three types of exceptional people who have an effect out of proportion to their number. Convert any one of these types to a "sticky" message, and they will share the message like a sneezer spreads a cold. We need to cultivate: connectors, mavens, and salesmen.

It can be difficult to recognize who these people are.

For those of us with retail specialty shops, there is one type of customer who fulfills all three roles: The Dedicated Self-Employed Professional. For some businesses, you can add The Extreme Hobbyist.

For my business, that customer is the Self-Employed Professional Housekeeper.

The professional housekeeper often has clients on a different social standing than she is; she "connects" different groups of people.

A dedicated professional housekeeper is always seeking more efficient ways to achieve the results her best-paying clients demand. Because of this, she becomes an information specialist, a maven.

Cleaning is survival for professional housekeepers. They are emotional about their cleaning equipment. Few ordinary people enthuse about their vacuum; most people save their excitement for important things like who won the World Series or the latest American Idol competition.

A dedicated housekeeper will break into a big grin or a glaring grimace when mentioning her vacuum. Her body language says more than any sales brochure ever will. Her emotional cues make her a compelling salesman for her vacuum beliefs. (S)he is a salesperson.

The dedicated self-employed professionals who patronize your business can have a larger accumulated affect on the success of your business than how much, where and how you advertise.

If any of your customers use your products as either an extreme hobbyist or as a self-employed professional, they can be the few who create the tipping point.

From the beginning, we did things to turn house-keeping ladies and men into our tipping-point sales force.

We tried to get them the best possible vacuum for their needs and budget, fix it when necessary, and even smile at them.

We do that much with all our customers.

It wasn't enough.

When you were dating the person you wanted to marry, did you treat that person any differently than your other friends?

Of course you did.

We needed to do more if we wanted to encourage each and every Dedicated Professional Housekeeper to be our active connector, maven and sales force.

We discovered following Grandma's advice was the best advice: Tell the truth.

We tell each self-employed professional cleaning person she/he is the most important part of our advertising budget.

When do we reveal this?

The moment we learn she is a professional housekeeper. If a customer is

Buying bags
Checking in a repair
Looking for a vacuum
and mentions cleaning homes for a living, we say:

"Did you know you are the most important part of our advertising budget?"

We give her time to react either verbally or nonverbally.

"I bet your friends ask for your cleaning advice all the time."

We wait for her to nod yes. If she goes into a story about people hounding her for advice, she's listened to intently. This lady is GOLD. Plus, listening shows respect.

Remember the sociologist's version of the Golden Rule: Whatever attitude you give to others is the attitude they give to—and about—you.

If we want to be remembered with respect and awe, we must respect our customers and find something special to admire about each one.

Each one of the professional cleaning people who come to my store inspires respect and awe. They are women and men who went out into a world of strangers and created their own employment. How could anyone not respect that?

The respect we give is returned.

Anyone who cannot find a reason to respect his customers, might be in the wrong business.

If when first meeting a new cleaning lady, she sings praises about a product we believe to be worthless, we do not immediately dump negativity on her.

Instead we state a positive truth, "You really care about the quality of work you do."

We wait for her to indicate that she cares a great deal about the quality of her work.

Then we confide, "Which is why your friends value what you have to say more than any advertisement we can buy. The EXTRA money I would have spent on advertising I spend directly with QUALIFIED Professionals such as yourself. Would you like to see how much quality you can get for your dollar here?"

Now is the time we can gently introduce choices other than what the customers has used. For anything contrary to her stated preferences we often say, "I once believed the same thing, but I have learned..."

The customer is intelligent, just without our depth of information and experience.

At all times we try to increase her self-confidence, especially when disagreeing with her.

No one is going to spread the word about us, our store or our vacuums if they harbor doubts about themselves. Or believe we insulted them.

After we solved the first problem that brought them into our store, we've done only half the job of making our store as contagious as a pet rock.

We've developed a messenger, but have given her a one note message and a one note reason to come to our store. It helped, but we need to get her to think of us more often.

We needed to make the message "stickier."

Cleaning ladies need to know how to get more work done in less time. Every time a professional can get a $10 service completed in half the expected time, that is like getting a $20/hour raise.

The more profitable a cleaning lady is, the more she will enjoy her work and the longer she will stay in the profession.

It is a lot easier to help the same person grow her business skills than to teach a new person the basics every two years.

Ask your Self-Employed Professionals, "What is the most time-consuming, difficult task you need to do?"

Keep written notes about these problems. This requires perseverance and frequent homework.

Whatever the cleaning professionals say is their biggest problem, we have studied to become helpful experts.

There is a fine line between being a braggart know-it-all and a friendly information source. Those times when we've crossed that line have had ugly results.

We've learned to avoid saying, "I know this is best!"

Instead, we say things like, "What my other professional clients have found that helps is..."

We keep a list of cleaning tips. I've learned to say, "Have you heard—?" and "Are you familiar with—-?" even when they come in to buy bags.

Unexpected cleaning tips are treated like valued presents. Your dedicated customers will use those tips to make their own services more valued.

Your customer becomes a resource to others, he is their "maven."

Every time someone asks him, "Which product do you prefer?" your customer becomes your outside salesman.

The more problems you have helped him solve, the "stickier" your store's message becomes.

Every time he conveys this information to someone who has not yet heard of your store, he has become your connector.

Your store has a good chance of becoming as contagious as a pet rock.

Your Most Important 60 Second Commercial

VARIATIONS OF THIS problem exist for all specialty businesses.

Has this ever happened to you?

You are at a social gathering and someone asks you The Question:

"What do you do for a living?"

You: "I have a vac shop."

"We just bought a new vacuum. It's the best one we ever had."

You (thinking one of <u>those</u> pieces of junk!): "Glad you like it. If it gives you trouble, bring it by."

"Not likely. We researched it really well." Sometimes he'll repeat how much they like their new vacuum, some will ask what you think about their new purchase. Others will start talking about every vacuum everyone in their family has ever owned.

The person has owned vacuums, uses them, therefore sees himself an expert on them. You do not seem useful.

Unless his new vacuum breaks down, he is no more likely to visit your store than if he had never met you.

It has happened to all of us.

We all want to generate new business.

We all have social opportunities to advertise our businesses to new people.

Many people think "vac dealer" means door to door salesman. "Vac shop" too often equates with old time fix-it shops. In a typical social encounter you have sixty seconds to change both impressions; to make "vac shop" suggest "valuable specialty store."

But, you want to behave in a socially acceptable manner. At the same time, you don't want to appear to endorse junk products.

Social networking sounds easy in theory, but the reality can be difficult.

There is a solution: Practice.

Most of us rehearse what we say to customers who come into our stores. We know the basic demo we give. We know the leading questions to ask our bag and belt customers to generate a demo, or at least future repair work.

When in our stores, we are on our own turf. We know the customer wouldn't be in a vacuum store if he didn't have a vacuum need.

It is just as important to practice what to say when away from our stores.

We each need a friendly sounding business description that doesn't sound like an advertisement—but is.

What should you say? That depends on your business's personality and how much time you will have to say it. It's a good idea to have a ten second, thirty second and full sixty second self-introduction. Write down several.

Read what you have written out loud.

Now you are ready to test how much your loved ones, love you. Read the self-descriptions you like best to your family. Ask them which ones make them think, "Wow, I'm glad your vac shops exist. It's the only place to buy a vacuum!"

Get their advice on how to make it better. If you have older children, make it a family project.

When you have your three self-introductions ready, it is time to practice.

How often should you practice?

Rehearse every morning while getting ready for work. Rehearse again every evening before going to bed.

Do it in front of a mirror, up close, watching your facial expressions. Then do it in front a full length mirror, critiquing your total body language.

Practice until the words sound as casual, and as easy, as "Hi, how are you?"

Don't worry about sounding too "canned." You will naturally make minor variations in different social situations. Don't worry about not being perfect. Your old teachers are not going to grade you.

What should you say? Whatever you believe is most important.

A few main points most include:

1 Positive reasons <u>WHY</u> you are in business, such as:

I've the pleasure of following my parents and grandparents...

We were lucky to get out of the corporate rat race...

My family wanted to own a business, and after exhaustive research we discovered...

2 Reasons why what you offer is not available elsewhere, examples:

People remember how their parents' vacuum lasted for ten years, yet they can't get one to last ten months. They come to my store to find out why.

Box stores are filling our land fills will stacks of disposable vacuums. It feels good to be able to offer people a quality product that the big corporations don't even want to make available.

There are so many people who live away from family members. It's good to be able to help both inexperienced young adults and the elderly with things like belt changes. Box stores sure don't care.

3 Your business name and where you are located by description.
Don't worry about exact address or hours. They just need enough information to look you up. If someone asks for your hours, you will know you have done a very good job in you sixty second commercial.
Examples:

Ever notice John's Vac shop across from the library? That's my shop.

Have you seen our new red sign on Sunset Boulevard, The Vac Shop?

We were lucky to find an excellent location in the Shopper's Plaza next to Tom's Pizza.

Does it matter which order you present these in? No.

One of my answers to "What do you do?"
"For going on thirty years, I've helped people with their vacuum needs. We've grown from just fixing vacuums, to a full cleaning solution store with more vacuum variety than the rest of the town put together."
Most will ask about which vacuum is best...

"There is no one best vacuum. We seek to educate people so they know what's important for their personal situation. That way you're not at the mercy of whoever has the biggest advertising budget."

I also vary my canned speech by the apparent social level of the person.

"I started in the vacuum business as a teenager earning money for college. After finally graduating, I discovered this business is a wonderful way to meet good people such as yourself."

The person will usually express surprise or a touch of disbelief...

"Think about your friends and relatives. Which ones care about doing a superior job cleaning their homes? That's the type who goes out of their way to go to a vacuum specialty shop. What other business automatically weeds out the riff-raft?"

Have fun advertising yourself!

I Lost a Sale Today

During tough economic times, it is too easy to become
our own worst selling handicap.

A PROMINENT BUILDER'S name flashed on my computer screen, along with a large sum of past-due money. For the past ten years he has always paid early, now he is over a month late. Why? Should I call him? Give him one more day?

I made the call. "Hi, how's it going? Is your client thrilled with his new built-in vacuum?" I learned the customer was happy with our vacuum installation, but unhappy with other aspects of his new home. The builder's customer is refusing payment until every problem's rectified.

"Some people are too picky for their own good. How about a partial payment to cover my installer's paycheck?"

He seemed relieved, and promised his wife would drop off a partial payment within the hour.

Next I reviewed accounts payable. Half were past due. I had counted on the builder's check to make them all current, but now... Should I pay a little on each? Pick only the oldest and pay that? Was there an insurance or tax payment due?

Knocking on my office door rudely interrupted my decision making.

"Fran, someone's here to buy a vacuum."

A new employee, she will get full credit for any sale we help her with.

I rushed out. "Hi, how are you."

The customer's friendly, answers all the questions about her vacuuming needs. My brain stays focused on the waiting paper work, not her answers.

Through out the demonstration, I recite features by rote instead of personalized benefits.

"You've given me a lot of information; I'll have to think about it." She leaves.

The new employee, "Wow, that was a great demo; I never knew so much about vacuums."

"That was one of the worst demonstrations I've given in a long time."

"But you showed how awesome that vacuum is."

"I recited facts. She would have saved time reading a brochure."

"But I thought we showed people the facts."

"But first we <u>Liston</u> to them. We personalize the information. She had a cleaning problem that drove her to come to a vac shop on a beautiful day. Instead of listening to her, showing her which vacuum could best solve <u>her</u> problems, I left my mind in the office with <u>my</u> problems."

She looked confused. I continued, "When someone walks in our door, our job is to help solve their **real problem**. When you go to a doctor because you think you have a cold, a good doctor doesn't assume you have diagnosed yourself correctly. He asks questions, examines you, attempts to find out what the real problem is.

"He concentrates on **you,** not his personal problems."

The Rest of the Story

The next day, the employee came running into my office. "She's back. She's still just looking, but has more questions."

A second chance!

I took a deep breath, praying, "Allow me to help this person."

I closed the office door both physically **and mentally**.

My only thought: "How can I best determine her cleaning desires, best match our products with her needs?"

With a relaxed grin, "Hi, how are you this beautiful morning."

A thousand dollars later, she left.

"Fran, you gave her so much more information yesterday. Today you just repeated her words, and said nothing new. Yet today she bought. Why?"

"Because today I listened to her; made her problems important. I explained every fact in terms of those problems. If I had focused on her yesterday like I did today, she would have bought yesterday."

Your Store: A Stage for a Great Performance!

WHEN SOMEONE ENTERS your store, he enters your theater.

Each employee is a performer; *every* item, a stage prop.

The first thing your customer notices is your store's cleanliness.

I went by the field of the slothful...it was all over grown with weeds....the stone wall ...broken down...so shall thy poverty come...(proverbs 24:30)

A trashed environment implies you are trash. Worse, just like sleazy looking theaters attract sleazier looking patrons, dirty stores attract questionable customers. Clean attracts people who value cleanliness.

Broadway producers know the right wardrobe can make a mediocre performance seem great. Wardrobe also defines your business.

The military, baseball teams, even the girl scouts, have uniforms. Shop uniforms increase a sense of belonging and tell the public "This person is special."

Even without shop uniforms, clothing choice tells the world how you want to be seen. Customers feel more at ease if they perceive you as being like themselves.

One of the easiest ways to do this is to dress like the people with whom you *most* want to do business. Politicians know this. That's why they wear cowboy hats in Texas and baseball caps in Minnesota.

You have a spotless, attractive business. You and your staff are dressed for success, but people don't buy from well-dressed mannequins.

Your most important need? A script!

It can be broad, general directions (like the so-called impromptu performances), or a detailed script.

You must know what it is you want the public to learn about your products, and share that knowledge with your employees. Just like a Broadway Theater rehearses, each of you must practice, Practice, <u>PRACTICE</u> your lines. Whenever there is a lull in business, even while stocking shelves, ask your employees (and yourself) questions a customer might ask.

Someone watching a Broadway play doesn't care if the leading lady has a headache or the villain a cold. He just wants entertainment. He'll tell everyone if the show was exceptionally bad or good. Mediocre is forgotten.

Likewise, if your customer leaves your shop feeling entertained (and better-than infomercial-educated), he **will** talk about you.

Bad experiences are also relived. Blah, ho-hum shopping is forgotten even faster than boring shows.

Like a curtain rises on Broadway, the front door to your shop opens...

Smile!

This is a modified abridgment from *Live Abundantly! Business Lessons from the Bible*, lesson 36, by Fran Tabor, available from Amazon.com and Kindle.

About the Author

FRAN HELPED START A two-person business in economically challenged Kalispell, MT.

The business grew from $20,000 per year to over $1,000,000 and two dozen employees. She strayed from what her parents taught her and from God's Word. She took personal credit for all her success.

Suddenly cancer & embezzlements wiped out all savings and left deep debt. Then the recession hit. Many small businesses around her died. Humbled, she returned to the values she had been taught. She survived. In time, her business again thrived. The principles shared in **Live Abundantly! Business Lessons from the Bible** are the secrets to her survival.

The fifteen attitude essays in this book are simply a few applications of basic business principles that have been practiced for thousands of years.

.

Don't miss out!

Visit the website below and you can sign up to receive emails whenever Fran Tabor publishes a new book. There's no charge and no obligation.

https://books2read.com/r/B-A-KKIU-ITXZB

BOOKS 2 READ

Connecting independent readers to independent writers.

About the Author

Fran loves laughter, learning, talking and writing -- sometimes all at the same time. She is often interviewed on podcasts, such as https://www.youtube.com/watch?v=8QLHmYgK9FE, where her part starts at 9:28.

Fran Tabor helped found a Mom & Pop Brick & Mortar business in 1978. Its first years it grossed less than $20,000 per year. It has survived divorce, embezzlements, cutthroat competition, uninsured cancer, recessions and rapidly changing technologies. From 2003 onward, it has grossed over a Million per year every year.

Read more at https://books2read.com/ap/8GkDdM/Fran-Tabor.